Texas, Being

Texas, Being

A State of Poems

EDITED BY
Jenny Browne

Maverick Books
TRINITY UNIVERSITY PRESS
San Antonio

Published by Maverick Books, an imprint of Trinity University Press
San Antonio, Texas 78212

The publisher has made every effort to contact rights holders for the poems
in this anthology. Rights holders for uncredited poems should contact the
publisher, and corrections will be made in a future printing of the book.

Cover design by DeuxSouth
Book design by BookMatters, Berkeley
Cover image: *Lasso No. 5*, by Minta Maria, mintamaria.com

978-1-59534-292-8 hardcover
978-1-59534-293-5 ebook

Printed in Canada

Trinity University Press strives to produce its books using methods and
materials in an environmentally sensitive manner. We favor working with
manufacturers that practice sustainable management of all natural resources,
produce paper using recycled stock, and manage forests with the best
possible practices for people, biodiversity, and sustainability. The press is
a member of the Green Press Initiative, a nonprofit program dedicated to
supporting publishers in their efforts to reduce their impacts on endangered
forests, climate change, and forest-dependent communities.

The paper used in this publication meets the minimum requirements of the
American National Standard for Information Sciences—Permanence of
Paper for Printed Library Materials, ansi 39.48–1992.

CIP data on file at the Library of Congress

28 27 26 25 24 | 5 4 3 2 1

CONTENTS

Texas, Being

A State of Poems

INTRODUCTION

She was *in a state*, one might say, to suggest strong feeling. Or *I state my case*, when we'd like to put something clearly and be heard. In music, too, one can state a theme or melody. Some of these poems are about the music of their languages. One concerns a hedgehog cactus, another a roller rink. From "Happy, TX" to "Palestine, Texas," and from seashores to skeletons to Selena. Some speak to our dead. Some to the sun. Others to the omissions of history. All are in one way or another *about* Texas, but as I like to tell my poetry students, good poems are always about more than one thing.

I borrowed the title for this book from the first poem I remember writing after arriving in the brutal and beautiful state I call home. My own poem is small in size, but she drives fast from human thirst to sharpened violence, from borders to allergies, from a far horizon toward a closer look at some roadkill.

Texas, Being

where blind catfish cruise
limestone caverns

from deeper we drink
while a man sweets tea

with his knife stirring
all the way down

border fires
making breathing a geography

mountain cedar
floating pollen fevers

bones in the road
sun bleached

possum grin just missing
the curb where she

like all the modern girls
paused to consider

her inventory of elsewhere
because we can

drive ten hours and some
how still be here

Ultimately, I believe this poem—like every poem in this book—is also about distance and intimacy, momentum and stillness, and all the inheritances and surprises of still being here.

And here too, here too, here too...

When I Stopped at the Exxon in Jourdanton

for Tom Walters, in memoriam

ROBERT A. AYRES

When I stopped at the Exxon in Jourdanton, where
blue men in plastic booths talk, or sip their coffee,
or spit tobacco in styrofoam cups, I thought of you

When I drove the patched roads past producing leases
with yellow flags Warning: Poisonous Gas,

And when I got to the farm, and the lock had been
changed, and I didn't have the key to get in,

And the roadrunner atop the gate post scampered
down and ran away clattering "Trespasser!
Trespasser!"

And I wrestled the welded gate from its hinge and
hobbled with its unsteady weight,

I saw how green the new leaves are—fresh as wounds;

I saw the string joining the furrows like suture led to
the wreckage of a homemade kite gone down;

I saw the mesquite split by the storm last summer late
open to the hard grain weathering, and I thought of
you

When the shrike snagged the rough-skinned lizard and
flew to the fence and skewered it there on a barb
like jerky to cure.

Happy, TX

CURTIS BAUER

Wrench clank, cotton dust, truck exhaust: these
are debts I've paid. The grass here so fragile
I need white gloves to touch it, and I touch

to believe. Geese fly beyond this south and the cold
settled around the lakeshores once they left. I'd stand
like a horizon to own a little space but I salvage

what I've lost by going back, root my feet in the earth,
hold fast to one place. Become part of the terrain.
   People
walk in woods, around tracks, and through pastures.

Only the poor like me stand still, even in our moving
there is slow standing—each step a slab of earth.
We own where we stand, where we squat. Here in

Happy I am iron until someone stops or looks long,
then I float and dissipate into red dirt dust. No one
mourns my leaving. I walk like dead weeds scatter.

Tumble away. But tumble slowly along ridge and
hollow and machine shop grit, rusty barrel dents,
the visiting whore's boa's shadow lifting and falling

in the wind, and scratching tires and pebble spatter of passing traffic heading away to own some other space. Where I stand is home. I own part of what I see.

The Saddest Song

after Townes Van Zandt

JAN BEATTY

If "Tecumseh Valley" is the saddest song ever written,
and if I'm writing out of my heart, and if

Townes really meant that . . . *sunshine walked beside her,*
then we're all fucked, and we are—

                and if

her dreams were denied / Her pa had died,
then I'm saying there's no season that's right

for dying, there's no weight that the heart
can make light, and I'll never see you again.

Snow Falling on Zebras

LAYLA BENITEZ–JAMES

Spain and Texas have some distance between them—
without a map I know this—you are ahead of me,
but I blink, and I am sure you are blinking now
it is 5:26 am
and i am in spain
Madrid in the center, Austin in the center—
it's impossible to pull up all the roots of want.

Westerns were filmed in Spain to echo Texas—
you showed me how a cloud could unzip my eye
and i love you
while, back home, snow fell on the neighbor's zebras,
and I missed it, as I am missing you now—
I want you to be walking with me.
Wild asters are everywhere because of the rain.

Texas

JORGE LUIS BORGES

Here too. Here as at the other
Edge of the hemisphere, an endless plain
Where a man's cry dies a lonely death.
Here too the Indian, the lasso, the wild horse.
Here too the bird that never shows itself,
That sings for the memory of one evening
Over the rumblings of history
Here too the mystic alphabet
Of stars leading my pen over the page to names
Not swept aside in the continual
Labyrinth of Days: San Jacinto
And that other Thermopylae, the Alamo.
Here too, the never understood
Anxious, and brief affair that is life.

The Yellow Rose of Texas

JENNY BOULLY

The Yellow Rose of Texas shines a color so bright it blinds all that Texas red and blue and white.

The Yellow Rose of Texas was never merely a rose; the Yellow Rose of Texas was a song; it was a woman; it was a girl.

In my elementary school cafetorium, the Yellow Rose of Texas was a girl with auburn hair and freckles.

The kindergarten classes are going to put on a show; the show will, in part, also teach us about Texas history, because in Texas, the history is unending.

On long strips of butcher paper, the Alamo we painted already grows old.

I'm as far away from the stage as possible.

I'm a lotus blossom; I'm a jasmine bud floating in water.

I wish it were me, the Yellow Rose of Texas.

I'm good at this: I know the songs by heart.

In my home, we fear the permission slip.

After school, my mother comes to pick us up and we go to a little pond off the highway, where we catch perch, and I throw spear grass into the grooves of trees. I sing and sing until the willows are dizzy that I am the Yellow Rose.

At school, I never sing. I only move my mouth like I am.

It's a cruelty, this circumstance in which I am never cast.

The other kids Mexican Hat Dance and hold such beautiful crinkly flowers, fuchsia and lime and turquoise dreams, and I myself fashioned one of those flowers, magenta and orange, a whole stack of tissue paper cinched together.

I thought I would be able to hold it, to take it home, to sing to it the song that only I, the half-child, knows.

No one told me it was merely a prop.

No one told me it was going to be stomped on and stomped on when it dropped.

Heart

CATHERINE BOWMAN

Old fang-in-the-boot trick. Five-chambered
asp. Pit organ and puff adder. Can live
in any medium save ice. Charmed by the flute
or the first thunderstorm in spring, drowsy
heart stirs from the cistern, the hibernaculum,
the wintering den of stars. Smells like the cucumber
served chilled on chipped Blue Willow. Her garden
of clings, sugars, snaps, and strings. Her creamy breasts
we called pillows and her bird legs and fat fingers
covered with diamonds from the mines in Africa.

The smell of cucumber... Her mystery roses...

Heading out Bandera to picnic and pick corn,
the light so expert that for miles
you can tell a turkey vulture
from a hawk by the quiver in the wing.
Born on April Fools', died on Groundhog's,
he pulls over not to piss but to blow away
any diamondback unlucky enough to be
on the road between San Antonio and Cotulla.

Squinting from the back of the pickup
into chrome and sun and shotgun confection,
my five boy cousins who love me more

than all of Texas and drink my spit
from a bottle of Big Red on a regular basis
know what the bejeweled and the gun-loading
have long since forgotten. And that is:
Snakes don't die. They just play dead. The heart
exposed to so many scrapes, bruises, burns,
and bites sheds its skin, sprouts wings and flies,
becomes the two-for-one sparkler on
the Fourth of July, becomes what's slung between
azure and cornfield: the horizon.

If you don't believe it
place your right hand on it
from the Pledge
like you've been taught.

Feel the hearing so deep. Limbless
and near limbless. Prefers the ambush
to the hunt. Sets a trap, picks a spot,
begins the vigil. Resorts at times to bluff
and temper. Swallows victims whole.
Tastes like chicken. Tastes like
hope, memory, forgiveness.

Better Than Paris

Good morning, I love you late   for a meeting
       I am still in bed our faces turned
to respective cardinal points south/north
if we are speaking only of heritage,   degrees of melatonin.

Architecture shapes the body

no matter the square footage, I feel   a thin frame
       around me, a 1920s duplex:
a thin white border
as in old photographs   around
       this middle-class winter.

I watch a shopping bag gallop
       down the middle of Ross Ave like some bad-ass cat.

Last night, looking for a parking space
       near the Dallas Public Library
I got lost, turned   right past
orange construction barrels, corporate headquarters,
county commissions, convention centers, turned
circles

in a downtown built in the late 1970s
       on the scale of a capital city
in some developing country, launched

like a wind-tossed plastic bag
                    into a future
at the farthest end of an uninterrupted plaza.

Door after glass door.
          Not a cop, not a vagrant in sight.

At the ruins of Pompeii, Melville writes
like any other town.   All the same
               whether one be dead or alive.
Pompeii comfortable sermon.

Last night, I dreamt I held a stone with an oyster shell
surface, some artifact of the soul
          5 years
the stone-shell gave me
                    existentially, perhaps geographically,
               perhaps I should stop worrying about my IRA.

          Melville liked Pompeii better than Paris.

The Germans have a word for this
feeling of walking across an interminably long space,
          this feeling
that we will never arrive at our destination: *platzangst.*

I watch a gray dove walk across Ross Avenue
in full morning   traffic.

If it's gray I call it a pigeon, even here in Texas,
walking across Ross Ave   as if it didn't have a wing
to its name.

One Day during the Pandemic, an Earth Day Poem

BOBBY BYRD

> Revolutionary consciousness is to be found among the most
> ruthlessly exploited classes: animals, trees, water, air, grasses.
> —*Gary Snyder*

One morning during the pandemic
springtime
the city silent with the fear of death
a hedgehog cactus from among its dangerous spines
gave birth to a single luscious pink and white blossom,
the size of a man's fist,
its sexual core bright yellow and gooey—
"the promised one,"
as stated in the prophecies.
The blossom, once born in the sunshine, began to
    preach
the gospel of the earth,
its dance through the wide blue sky,
the sermon explaining
exactly
how and why humanity is not needed,
if it ever was, thank you,
for the earth, sun, moon, and sky,

the great boundless universe,
to flourish
in the truth of love.
All day long the flower preached,
interrupted from time to time
by a pair of black-chinned hummingbirds,
seasonal migrants from south to north,
who kept coming by
greedy for communion, the body and blood,
take this and eat, take this and drink.
There was that one black bumblebee too,
squat little beast,
ravaging the delicate core of the flower's being.
The flower continued its sermonizing
unperturbed
while attending to these duties.
Neighbors and friends,
walking up and down the street,
stopped by to experience first hand
the flower's message.
What they learned, only time will tell.
We'll see, won't we?
The flower preached until sunset
and during twilight it slowly
closed those delicate petals into itself,
packed its bag and disappeared
forever. The cactus
didn't seem to mind. It had small buds

already perched among its spines,
each with its own truth to tell—
in its own time, of course,
the long hot summer, the winter to come.

Something about Texas

CHRISTOPHER CARMONA

There's something about Texas,
rolling through these towns preserved like a gift shop
    postcard.
I feel the slowness of time,
the bustle of a town on the brink of decay.
Like a Larry McMurtry novel
the only constant is the single Mexican restaurant
                              where all the trucks gather.

Blue Celestial

ALINE B. CARTER

There is a flower on the Texas plains,
Ethereal as dawn, in pearly blue
It must have caught the morning skies when rains
Had passed in misty showers, where it grew.
So much it is a part of highest Heaven
When petals turn, unfolding to the light,
It seems to be a strange mysterious leaven
Transmuting lowly earth. For just the sight
Is love—and beauty, fragile as a breath—
Men call it Blue Celestial, wondering why
It fades into a dewy mist at death,
As though to blend again, into the sky.

Borderline

ROSEMARY CATACALOS

South Texas car ashtrays are kept full of change,
coins to pave the way across the river and back.
Going either direction we fix our eyes
on that elusive spot somewhere up ahead
where everything comes together,
the kind of border we all want.
Like old Yousuf Assad in the dying downtown,
who keeps selling cheap plastic lace
Last Supper tablecloths to send money home:
the matter of a sister who never married.
Here he lives out his summer figs, the stunted
cedar at his door, force-feeding them on memory.
Try telling *him* about borders, that someday you look
across the distance and, sure enough, the big things
are closer, the small things farther away.
He wants to believe you, has staked a lifetime
on the possibility of just this
perspective. Same as the rest of us at Pappas's
godforsaken dustbin of a café, all the pies
raisin until we look hard and see the flies move.
We look hard, for all the good
it does, then go on faith. I tell you, brother,
we're made to show ourselves, act like we know

what we're doing. So great is our need that, if we got
our hands on the stars, we'd bite down on them like
    coin,
and even if they proved counterfeit,
tender their wholesale brightness for safe passage.

Marfa, Texas

VICTORIA CHANG

Here, there are grasses rolled
into dry moons, then carted
off on trailers to the edge of
the rain. Here, there is so
much sky that even birds

get lost. Oh to be loved the
way the day loves the night.
See how slowly they
separate? All day long the
trees move, each leaf in a

different direction, as if by
the work of fingers on a body.
How many times our bodies
imagined by another mind.
How many times the day

imagined the night. Once I
loved a man so much that
when he didn't love me back,
I closed my eyes and drank a
whole bottle of night.

How I felt night rush into my
body, then out through my
skin as envelopes. At the
time, I only felt pain but years
later, all I remember is joy,

the kind of love that seems
grinded off of a moon.
Perhaps such love cannot
ever be returned, just
returned in the imagination.

The Symbolic Life

HAYAN CHARARA

They kept showing up, for days,
dead on the windowsill,
and for days I did nothing about the ladybugs
except to ask if their entering the house
unnoticed and dying before I saw them
was symbolic.
Thinking so was easy.
They symbolized birth and death,
change and rebirth.
It was also possible the tiny beetles
embodied an inborn need
to show themselves,
to turn up in every and any place,
even as the dried out remains of the once lively.
Or they stood for the burden of being one thing
relieved by becoming another,
which all the world's children suffer.
This went on and on, and could've gone on
forever, so finally I opened the window
and blew them into the wide open
because everything and everyone should get a chance
to be mourned, and they got theirs,
but first they had to die, which is life,
not symbolism.

My Father at 32

JOSHUA EDWARDS

Early one June morning, 1978,
the photographer stands alone
on a Texas beach several days
before his first child will be born,
ten years removed from an
extended tour in Vietnam.
Through his camera he sees
ships, oil platforms, stone and
wood piers, clouds dissipating
as they move, swells becoming
surf, the sun low on the horizon
in the east. In his satchel are
lenses and a book on mythology.
He never forgets what he reads.
Also in his head is a crystalline
idea for the life he wants to live,
one which cannot be planned but
must be self-determined.
He is tall, handsome, and looks
older than his age, his hair slowly
going gray since twenty. After
the war, he hitchhiked across
the country, working odd jobs
and having strange adventures,

all the time thinking about war,
fear, superstition, and oblivion.
He looks around. Surfers are
getting their boards out of vans
and a few old couples stroll along
the seawall behind him. He turns
back to face the water and takes
several photographs of waves.

Aubade: Summer, Texas

TARFIA FAIZULLAH

Long planks of sky narrow, then widen
like your mother's saris whipped out
and over the banks of the old fish pond.
You are in the backyard, alone, Father,

the faint scent of coriander still lingering
on your fingers...Life is always refined
by prayer—you've told me this for years.
Can you feel, anymore, the soil between

your fingers? You kneel anyway, pull away
hearts of knotweed from rows of your garden.
Neither the sky nor your hands will change
what they do—you lay out the prayer mat

on summer grass. You cannot stop looking
for the face of the god who, even at dawn, is silent.

Ode at Skateland Texas

CARRIE FOUNTAIN

To the six-year-old
in the black denim
jumper and strict

bangs and skates that
light up and flash
radically, who

maintains a perfect
equilibrium
by appearing to be

falling at all times.
Oh being propelled
by a joy entirely

your own, falling
and falling and falling
forward. Let no one

on Earth tell you
that you aren't doing
everything right.

Still Life with Summer Sausage, a Blade, and No Blood

VIEVEE FRANCIS

*East Texas, 198_*

I remember, we walked (we didn't walk)
from the farmhouse to the store in Palestine
(we drove the truck, got out, went in).
The storefronts hadn't changed since
my father was a child. He grabbed saltines from the bin
(he brought a box) and he bought some sausage.
We walked (yes, then we walked) around town
as we ate (he shared). He gave me some summer
sausage, cut with his pocket knife. I pulled the pieces
from the point of the blade. I knew (knew)
nothing would happen (though he was silent)
to alter this memory. We were together
in Texas and we ate and walked in silence
and it felt like smiling, like skipping, like saying
"Daddy," and him not minding, not minding at all.

Dear Chaos

MAG GABBERT

In Lubbock I used to find severed wings
in the parking garage—pigeons, I think.
It was as if the wind had snapped them off.
I used to watch walls of dust blow across
the horizon; rain the color of blood,
rust, mud. I know you're not the same as God.
You don't have the same wrath my grandma once
said causes plagues. Maybe that's why I want
your help instead—because I bet you would
just toss a coin. I trust your indifference.
Besides, I'm not that religious. Unless
you count me asking mercy for the dead.
Or count the way I hold my hands, hidden
behind my back, at least two fingers crossed.

A Heron's Age

MIRIAM BIRD GREENBERG

The moon lies awake all night, peering down
through pecan canopy. The familiar is no longer:
   barred owl

that's built a nest at the base of a tree in the yard,
around which a round wire fence meant to contain

not her, but a white dog who would do her harm,
   who inhabits
all out-of-doors his chain can orbit, parabola brief

as the breadth of his explorations, or
if shirked, he roves the countryside, losing

his own way home until my brother leaves off circling
   the fields
in a combine, or his field-side mechanic's truck,

to find this animal half as large as either of us,
   cowering
lost in a ditch where a great blue heron shot by a
   hunter

laid down the tasseled strands of its head to die
ten years before. I've gone so far from home, even the
   owls

are unknown to me. Even the purple-lobed vetch
and the low place in the grass where, longer ago than a
     heron's life-

span, a black kid goat lay newly buried under packed
     dirt,
and longer before that when I lived, every afternoon

for a summer, in a child's hideout woven for me of
     branches
by a woman who today talks to demons from outer
     space, is dying

of breast cancer or curing it by meditating
to exorcism videos, she tells me. Everything I know

is hidden like a caul over the moon means rain, a
     gesture
at forgetting in service of something better. Put up

like a jar and forgotten until, dark as peaches
preserved by a great aunt three decades gone and even
     longer

from the house where she did her canning, I find and
     marvel
at it as if I were a child in an abandoned cellar. We are
     decay-

ing second by second, and certainty, so within
reach a heron's age ago, is a winged animal glimpsed

above in the unstitched dark. It knows nothing
of humanness; if it senses me, it is brief as its shadow

passing above through the night, but I name it
a benediction in the instant before it's gone.

Lonestar

LUCY GRIFFITH

I am a place to live widely
and here I'm not bragging

I'm the best place to find
what's on the far side
of far

yet my star sags
fear-tarnished   with bullies

dulling my shine
still each of my towns
hides a café with the same menu

a table of wisdom   old men
fragrant with coffee and stories

once thought of as haven
for those different
now banning   choice   thought   books

my skies are unbroken
a river joining east and west
a flyway welcoming

migrants with wings
whooping crane
goose   hawk   sparrow

the sun ascends   then rests
on all my edges
bejeweled

with ridiculous colors
my skies even now the deepest
the darkest

my people at their best
when the weather's gone to hell

One Year in Texas

AARON HAND

my texas skeleton sunburned & blistered beige
my texas skeleton slouched toward the bethel birdbath
   long dried up
my texas skeleton swam in cumulus shadows
my texas skeleton wove a sweater out of the fog &
   wore it like an evening offering
my texas skeleton forgot all about its summer skin
so the wind whispered last rites to my texas skeleton
and it hibernated in the crown of an unrelenting
   snowstorm
my texas skeleton groveled at frostbitten feet
until my texas skeleton was lifted up by the rising sun
it bathed in the rain & the rain & the rain
called cankerworms to inch my collarbone until
my texas skeleton bloomed in waves of violet

Palestine, Texas

FADY JOUDAH

"I've never been," I said to my friend who'd just
come back from there. "Oh, you should definitely
go," she said. "The original Palestine is in Illinois."
She went on, "A pastor was driven out by Palestine's
people and it hurt him so badly he had to rename
somewhere else after it. Or maybe it goes back to
a seventeenth-century Frenchman who traveled
with his vision of milk and honey, or the nut who
believed in dual seeding." "What's that?" I asked.
"That's when an egg is fertilized by two sperm," she
said. "Is that even viable?" I asked. "It is," she said,
"on rare occasions, though nothing guarantees the
longevity of the resulting twins." She spoke like a
scientist but was a professor of the humanities at heart.
"Viability," she added, "depends on the critical degree
of disproportionate defect distribution for a miracle
to occur. If there is life, only one twin lives." That
night we went to the movies looking for a good laugh.
It was a Coen brothers feature whose unheralded
opening scene rattled off Palestine this, Palestine that
and the other, it did the trick. We were granted the
right to exist. It must have been there and then that
my wallet slipped out of my jeans' back pocket and

under the seat. The next morning, I went back. With a flashlight that the manager had lent me I found the wallet unmoved. This was the second time in a year that I'd lost and retrieved this modern cause of sciatica in men. Months earlier it was at a lily pond I'd gone hiking to with the same previously mentioned friend. It was around twilight. Another woman, going in with her boyfriend as we were coming out, picked it up, put it in her little backpack, and weeks later texted me the photo of his kneeling and her standing with right hand over mouth, to thwart the small bird in her throat from bursting. If the bird escapes, the cord is severed, and the heart plummets. She didn't want the sight of joy caught in her teeth. He sat his phone camera on its pod and set it in lapse mode, she wrote in her text to me. I welled up. She would become a bride and my wallet was part of the proposal. This made me a token of their bliss, though I am not sure how her fiancé might feel about my intrusion, if he would care at all. "It's a special wallet," I texted back. "It's been with me for the better part of two decades ever since a good friend got it for me as a present." "He was from Ohio," I turned and said to my film mate who was listening to my story. "Ohio?" She seemed surprised. "Yes," I replied quizzically. "There's also a Palestine in Ohio," she said. "Barely anyone lives there anymore. All of them barely towns off country roads."

Fore Tell

JIM LaVILLA-HAVELIN

our front lawn
cenizo
        brought home from Alpine
        seasons ago
                        and still thriving
goes a perfect purple
a dusty lavender
against thin green
                        when rain is coming

desert sage
knows what will come
        more accurate than
        a finger in the wind
        or whether the cows
        are sitting or standing

less painful than
waiting to feel it
in my bones

In Exile

EMMA LAZARUS

> Since that day till now our life is one unbroken paradise. We
> live a true brotherly life. Every evening after supper we take
> a seat under the mighty oak and sing our songs.
>   *—excerpt from a letter by a Russian refugee in Texas*

Twilight is here, soft breezes bow the grass,
Day's sounds of various toil break slowly off.
The yoke-freed oxen low, the patient ass
Dips his dry nostril in the cool, deep trough.
Up from the prairie the tanned herdsmen pass
With frothy pails, guiding with voices rough
Their udder-lightened kine. Fresh smells of earth,
The rich, black furrows of the glebe send forth.

After the southern day of heavy toil,
How good to lie, with limbs relaxed, brows bare
To evening's fan, and watch the smoke-wreaths coil
Up from one's pipe-stem through the rayless air.
So deem these unused tillers of the soil,
Who stretched beneath the shadowing oak tree, stare
Peacefully on the star-unfolding skies,
And name their life unbroken paradise.

The hounded stag that has escaped the pack,
And pants at ease within a thick-leaved dell;
The unimprisoned bird that finds the track
Through sunbathed space, to where his fellows dwell;
The martyr, granted respite from the rack,
The death-doomed victim pardoned from his cell,—
Such only know the joy these exiles gain,—
Life's sharpest rapture is surcease of pain.

Strange faces theirs, wherethrough the Orient sun
Gleams from the eyes and glows athwart the skin.
Grave lines of studious thought and purpose run
From curl-crowned forehead to dark-bearded chin.
And over all the seal is stamped thereon
Of anguish branded by a world of sin,
In fire and blood through ages on their name,
Their seal of glory and the Gentiles' shame.

Freedom to love the law that Moses brought,
To sing the songs of David, and to think
The thoughts Gabirol to Spinoza taught,
Freedom to dig the common earth, to drink
The universal air—for this they sought
Refuge o'er wave and continent, to link
Egypt with Texas in their mystic chain,
And truth's perpetual lamp forbid to wane.

Hark! through the quiet evening air, their song
Floats forth with wild sweet rhythm and glad refrain.

They sing the conquest of the spirit strong,
The soul that wrests the victory from pain;
The noble joys of manhood that belong
To comrades and to brothers. In their strain
Rustle of palms and eastern streams one hears,
And the broad prairie melts in mist of tears.

Independence Day in West Texas

J. ESTANISLAO LOPEZ

Bought with the soiled coins
I pinched from the floorboard of our father's truck,
my sister's sparkler fell into her sandal.
Below her body,
light pooled against desert night—
a coincidence of beauty and suffering,
which I would learn is an old coincidence.
Old, too, a boy's hands placed
on the causal chain.
My mother smothered the glowing lace,
first with her hands,
then with a towel my brother fetched.
Fireworks continued.
Horned lizards skittered beneath wood pallets.
I sunk behind our Dodge, and, as my sister cried out
to a luminous sky I then believed was listening,
I buried my legs in gravel,
counting seconds between its shifts of hue.
After the fireworks, gunfire resounded,
continuing through my sleep. I dreamt explosions
turning milky, flooding the desert,
saturating it—
our feet steeped in the milk, my sister's and mine

together. Then, others' feet: our countrymen,
who pledged this precise disaster:
that for her woundedness she'd be remembered,
for her woundedness she'd be loved.

Texas

excerpt

PRIMO FELICIANO MARÍN DE PORRAS

Hail Texas, fraught with charms unknown
To every land beside;
By Nature's fairest traits is shown
In thee creation's pride;
As if the latest touch essay'd
By hand of Him the world Who made
Thy region beautified.
When resting to pronounce it good
Complacently His work He view'd.

I see thy plains of waving green
All flower-enamel'd spread
To where the morning's ruddy sheen
Is thence upon them shed—
It awes my soul as when I view
The summer sea's expansive blue
While ruffling winds are dead—
So calm, so vast, so fair to see,
A type of God's immensity.

But ere thy day-beam meets the eye
Upon the prairie's breast,
And earlier glowing golds on high

The Sierra Madre's crest.
To him whose feed the cliffs explore
Out peeping veins of precious ore
That region's wealth attest;
And gray embowered rocks unfold
Their specks and winding threads of gold.

Gone Yanaguana

PABLO MIGUEL MARTÍNEZ

It was a generous prayer,
a mother's gushing—full
and sweet and cool.
      She opened
her brown mouth when we
needed her blessing most.
      Too long
in the bone-colored light
we walked, so much
      mean dust
hid the way ahead, what was
to be. Her murmur brought us
here—

Come and kiss this wildgrass
place, this shimmeringfish
place. This friendly clearwater.
      This answering
      place.

Here she would stay, she said,
her songwords swimming,
endless,
      if we listened,
if we guarded and watched.

But I augur
other ways.
The stars' dance, wanton,
in the skies beyond: In a cracked-
lip, wicked-wind time, her stirred
waters will make
stomachs twist as limbs
in a loudvoice blowing.
And after
we are bent like wood, a clan
of tall, thirsty ghosts will tame
the wild flow.
This I see.
Then, after
many bison runs, it will go
dry—the gurgle stilled,
the flowering
gone.
Throats will ache, the heartplace, too,
from blood-making thorns.
When many leaves
separate from their mothertrees,
it all will cease. They will wonder,
some ones to come, how the
clearwater trickled
to a dream far and ash-smeared,
foul and selfish.
Gone the streaming
prayer. Gone forever.
Gone Yanaguana.

Wishing for More Than Thunder

WALTER McDONALD

Mirages hover like angels fanning the fields.
We see them in summer, a shimmer of wings.
Our stubborn steers ignore them, wading dry areas.
They hook their horns in invisible robes,

shaking their heads to graze. For them,
the sky is falling, the grass is manna.
Having lost all hope when they entered
the round corral as calves, they stuff themselves

with grass even in drought, as if all pastures
of the world were theirs. They never wonder
if God's in His heaven. Stubble is heaven enough,
alfalfa paradise. Watching steers graze

in a lake of shimmering light, seeing angels
fanning themselves, we wonder if even they
could make it rain, how many spin on a windmill,
how many squeezed would make a decent cloud.

In the Texas Summer Heat

JASMINNE MENDEZ

Humidity sucks the throat
fantasmas & vírgenes bless
a kick of feet
beneath the dinner table

she tells me   cuentos
I was never meant to hear

love notes passed at school
rumors like roaches scurry
scratched on paper napkins
between tattered sheets of linen

he wrote me into   poems &
I never read aloud

head down, eyes averted
soft feet make no sound
steam inside a kettle
out of boiling rooms

her body breathes
waiting to be found

bulletproof candelabras   &
I don't like secrets either

but around every corner
Lucy sells her body
Tito raped a girl &
a mami cheated on a papi

relentless words heard
his body muffles   pain

out of heavy chests
rapid heartbeat pumps
palms begin to sweat
blushing without finesse

waiting to be   found
her body breathes   itself

out of boiling rooms
steam inside a kettle
soft feet make no sound
head down, eyes averted

blushing without finesse
palms begin to sweat
rapid heartbeat pumps
out of heavy chests

his body muffles   pain
linen
relentless
a mami cheated on a papi
Tito raped a girl
Lucy sells her body
around every corner

& I don't like secrets either but
humidity   sucks
the throat

I never read aloud
he wrote me into poems &

scratched on paper napkins
between   tattered sheets of
rumors like roaches scurry
love notes passed at school

I never should've heard
she tells me   cuentos

'neath the table
a kick of feet   silenced
fantasmas & vírgenes bless
bulletproof   candelabras
          in the Texas summer heat

A Letter from Texas

excerpt

TOWNSEND MILLER

John it is a strange land. John it is hard to describe.
But perhaps like this: hold up your right hand, palm
    outward
And break the last three fingers down from the joint
And there I think you have it. The westering thumb
The beautiful bleak land, the silent mesas
Big Bend and the great canyons and at its end
El Paso, the Northern Pass, and they came down
    through it.
Southward and east the slow hot river moving
River of Palms, Grande del Norte, and over the wrist
To Brownsville and it empties in the vast blue waters.
Upward the long coast curving and far above it
Over the bent joints the red bordering river
Red River, land of the Washita and Tejas
And last the index, Panhandle, the high plains
The bleached bone laid on the huge heart of the
    continent.
This is the empire; this is the hand flung out
The large western dream and the tongue staggers
To speak it for the size or where to take it.

Lean Steer

ANGE MLINKO

What's with the antique stores, the butterflies
and sunflowers rigged from scrap metal?
The sempiternal biergarten (alias
saloon) with its wide screens (football),

a spice-grinding abandon to the windup radio's
right-wing warm-ups? The hog-callin'
melismas of the local girl star's now going, *Adios*.
Where the tin flower's rust is read as pollen.

[Rosenberg, TX]

Texas Remedy

NAOMI SHIHAB NYE

Step outside at twilight,
this sky won't wait.

Crushed wrapper blowing down the street—
release what snares you—then go chase that trash.

Answer rising egret with your own breath.
Yes, it's terrible, but the sky still looms

larger than any place you ever called
home. Remember what a door was for,

letting in people you love,
swinging wide still, when no one is there

and little recognized. Now it's the wind's turn.
In Texas, always a wide chill coming

to change the sky before the ground.
Be patient, sure there's lots of bad around,

but more room for good too, with all this empty.
Goats that don't freeze, thirsty rivers,

Ozona, Electra and Alice, bearing
their own sorrows and staggering joys.

Blow a kiss to the far-off town
of your first real job,

Longview.
Pretend it branded you.

A Day without an Immigrant, Dallas, Texas

SHIN YU PAI

At Pearl Street station,
two brown-skinned men

in painter's pants stand
out in a sea of white

I am just one more face
sticking out in a crowd

& it is my privilege

that prevents me from
understanding why

the workers want to know
how to buy one-way trips

the automated machine
sells only one roundtrip fee,

back to where you came from

he isn't asking me for change
says it clear enough so that

there can be no mistake
Sí. Yo sé.

But a dollar fifty is a lot of money.

Texas Natives

CECILY PARKS

Apache plume
Mexican blazing star
Blue agave
Cherokee sedge
Mexican devilweed
Mexican elderberry
Esperanza
Fall obedient plant
Mexican feathergrass
Gaura
Mexican hat
Indian blanket
Jimsonweed
Mexican juniper
Kingcup cactus
Lluvia de oro
Mexican marigold
Mexican navelwort
Oreja de ratón
Mexican panicgrass
Queendevil
Red-spike Mexican hat
Mexican silktassel

Mexican thistle
Uña de gato
Vela de coyote
Mexican weeping juniper
Xcanchac-che
Mexican yellowshow
Hierba del cáncer
Zitherwood

[The Gulf doesn't miss us]

EMMY PÉREZ

The Gulf doesn't miss us. The redfish don't nor do the speckled trout. I miss everything about the beach and its reasons for existing which are simply that it does. Shore sand packed down by waves and pressed with footprints till it smooths again and ghost crab burrow drops. Dunes covered with beach morning glories and railroad vines, platicando, till they close up for rest.

That we no longer recreate is the pandemic black hole swallowing homes whole as we continue: mess and clean our living space, mess and clean. You say I exaggerate, an exaggeration. Isn't the Gulf an exaggeration, with its dolphins and blue man o'war siphonophores, its seaweed and Space X debris? Elucidate, don't exonerate. Celebrate what lives and fight fuckery. Is ecstasy without drugs an exaggeration?

Hombres

OCTAVIO QUINTANILLA

The fields vibrating with buckshot, evening
     like a horsetail, trailing the light's dim promise.
My uncle brings home the half-open mouth
     of a white-tailed deer, the rest of its body
follows, antlers heavy
         like a wooden cross.
I am small, press myself against my father's legs,
     the massive animal on the table
someone built sturdy for times like these.
Under the lightbulb gently swaying in the humid air,
     the men drink beer
and point to the only star willing to testify
     on their behalf.
I am curious about death, but I've never seen
     the meadows where the grown men go,
never alone to rub wilderness
         all over my arms and chest.
Staring into the buck's dead eyes,
     I know I will be alone one day,
     in a field all atremble with evening,
the dying light's bristle against my face,
     the torsos of the men who loved me
     laced with the earth's skin.

Another Selena Poem

ILIANA ROCHA

Oh, oh, baby: the door opened making new, irregular
air, startled into the shape of Texas. Blood behind each
    syllable,
as if my body recognized touch & pulse before a hand
had ever laid there. She made love to vowels while I

hated the sound of my own name, each *i* & *a*
their own kind of irrevocable aches. She turned *Iliana*
inside out, stretched it into something almost
delicate but still strange. *Amor prohibido*: nothing less
    than

homesickness & its inverse—the more cumbia,
the further language ran from me. More ranchera,
    closer
she came. Distance between unfamiliar & familiar
shorter than a bullet's reach, light tripped over light to
    warm

her silhouette in wounds, & something about her ass
that's already been said a million times & better.

Rosary Beads

ANDREA "VOCAB" SANDERSON

I have no rosary beads to rub in supplication to the
patron saint of lost things.
But I offer this psalm to a risen king in the thanks for
   my city.
My city, San Antonio is gathered here like hands
clasping together in prayer
and song from the tip top of a needle point towering
heights above our heads,
to the basin of the blue hold that still babbles
hallowed words of Yanaguana.
We are a fiercely loving city tougher on the outside
but smooth as pecan shells.

To the South

IRE'NE LARA SILVA

> Researchers estimate that five thousand to ten thousand
> people escaped from bondage into Mexico.... There's
> some evidence that *tejanos*, or Mexicans in Texas, acted
> as "conductors" on the southern [Underground Railroad]
> route by helping people get to Mexico.
> —*Becky Little*

I imagine a light. A solitary light.
No voices. Only a beckoning hand.
I imagine children waking up wide-eyed
to see strangers asleep beside them
on the floor, a little girl holding tight
to a rag doll just like theirs.

1850—Alabama, Georgia, Mississippi,
South Carolina, and Virginia—
reported more than 300,000 people enslaved
in their states. Freedom was not the North.
Freedom was Canada. Freedom was Mexico.
Northern states were not freedom while the
Fugitive Slave Acts were law.

I imagine kind voices speaking Spanish
and even then, the Native-touched Tex-Mex

of the region. Offering water, coffee, a hot
tortilla off the comal. I imagine them
communicating with hand signals. I
imagine a plate of pinto beans, nopales,
rabbit in mole, arroz con pollo,
carne guisada tasted for the first time.
I imagine a sudden smile and a belly
sighing in relief at the ceasing of its hunger.

Mexico abolished slavery in 1829 and then
refused to sign any agreements that would
allow for the return of those who'd found
freedom on Mexican soil. So the Underground
Railroad developed a southern route. Through
Texas, through the Rio Grande Valley. Yes,
even through Texas, a land that so tenaciously
clung to its desire to enslave that it seceded
from two countries to do so—
Mexico in 1836 and the U.S. in 1861.

I imagine many homes with a light at
the window. Many kind faces. Many plates
of food. Many blankets. Many guides in the night
helping those who needed help through the
darkness, through the wild, across rivers, away
from unjust laws, away from enslavement, away.

I imagine it as it has always been and rarely recorded.

At Our Disposal

JEFF SIRKIN

I'm always coming up short, on my knees, peeking
through the glass at the progress on the empty house
next door. Sagging shelves and appliances in the
driveway, birds popping in and out of the sage out
front, blooming purple, the recently bared roots in
the yard plotting their way under the foundation,
under the soiled carpets and the discarded satellite dish
and the light streaming in. There's a word for that,
something about all this noise weaponized against us,
this slow asphyxiation called screen time. I try to find
the definition, the company logos flickering faster
than the eye can see. The wings of an owl, the belly
of a penguin, the nose of a kingfisher, the idea and the
process sliding with me into the dispose-all. There's
black smoke rippling over the border for the third time
in three days, and while we weren't looking the girls
next door disappeared. So where do we go to treat all
these wounded, the child soldiers hiding behind their
weapons in the playground? And when we rise, what
world will we slip on, tilting into the wind? There
is no order to what we might lose there, the layered
surfaces and their treasures caught up in the breeze, a
fortune in backlit devices. The playmates are jumping

into the water, hand-in-hand, again and again. But
these are the words to be used as evidence, all this torn
flesh born into its own smoldering transfiguration,
these hazy pictures bleeding into the cloudless sky.

This place on earth

MARGO TAMEZ

"won't be paved under by plunder"
and this is how my mother was the first oral
historian I knew, and she taught me poetry and history
are first cousins from the same clan.

Storying kónitsáá* when I was a girl sitting at the
    kitchen table,
she flapping tortillas on the flat cast iron,
I was the child eager to hear stories of old village
    gossip,
legends, spats, conflicts, and forgiveness by the river.

"The river is our life," I heard more often over the
    decades, she
voicing reliance and confidence in ways I struggled to
    know.
She was the oldest living survivor of warriors, and
    Elders sang
the lightning down to her hands when she was five,

*Rio Grande river

encoding her with escape routes and surviving wars.
    My next-gen body
only remembered dislocations, internal checkpoints,
    disconnections,
and a gulag wall. When I left Texas, I gradually
    rekindled her embers
of storytelling and oral history, and far away from
    Texas I needed her

storying of our village and other Ndé* villages in
    kónitsáá, and I have a
feeling her stories are like Indigenous long poems. She
    wanted me
to get this on my own. Over years she nudged me to
    write, to read.
Fought battles against principals and superintendents.
    Labored

for books, pencils, paper, dictionaries, and new
    chances.
I visited the village many times growing up, though
    couldn't imagine
what life was before big wars against Ndé, and big
    wars against

*the people / Lipan Apache

villages in other places on earth. When I got much
    older, she told me I was

getting closer to learning about her birthplace, a place
    the men of the first
war clad in armored, metal skins renamed El Calaboz
    in their language.
The dungeon.
Once, during a pause in a story, I watched the blue
    pulse in a thin vein at her

wrist quickening, and she said, "the Ndé gokíyąą"*
    will remain like flows in
rivered remembering, rivered secreting, and rivered
    archiving everything
we hold inside the pomegranate of our being. When I
    was a young girl
chasing grasshoppers down at soil level, five-foot-high
    Johnson grass

and Indian gum plants nested the backyard of our
    rental HUD row house
on Glendora Street, in San Antonio on the fringe of
    Fort Sam Houston. Far away
from the village, the pollen intellect of my being woke
    me to daily passages

*country / homeland

of a Southern Pacific train chugging down the track a
     few yards from our

back stoop. When I was older, I learned the train
     hauled extractions from
South Texas and the Rio Grande Valley up to the
     Dakotas and Canada, though
when younger, this happened while I hid in weeds,
     with grasshoppers. Much
older, I moved to Canada, after the extractions left
     death scapes, and my

storying about the wall resulted in nonvoluntary exile.
     It was true her
stories brought me home to Ndé kónitsáá gokíyąą, and
     poetry and history
are first cousins from the same clan, and this
place on earth won't be plundered because we remain.

Jesus in Cowboy Boots

for Colton

LORETTA DIANE WALKER

I don't know if it was a Tuesday or Wednesday
when dawn cracked the darkness
and fell into the wide open road of morning

a perfect offering,
like my friend's freckles-less son.

Veined with shadows of telephone wires
he slanted his face upward,
shut his eyes, unsealed the smile on his lips.

Look, Mama. I'm Jesus!
With arms extended, his babyish body
was an imperfect crucifix.

Sun-spikes nailed his hands to air.
Cowboy boots anchored him
to the top of a slide.

Robed in his daddy's T-shirt,
his dispensation was tasting
the warmth of a blue West Texas day.

A skinny wind rose like an omen,
blew gently across his open hands,
as light hung on him beneath an ebullient sky.

Uvalde

EMILY WINAKUR

What I remember of Uvalde is their debate team,
a girl with a snakeskin briefcase.
The name, a jewel in the mouth, like others—
    Guadalupe, Bandera—
redolent of sky, space, heat, the sense of a journey,
    roads turning and turning.
What I saw when I looked out the window of the car
was an example, in landscape form, of all I could do
    and be.
I rarely thought about my parents' gun, zipped in its
    holster,
invariably locked in a glove box.
Sometimes, when I was scared at night, listening to
    wind or coyotes,
I considered its uselessness.
Other people kept their guns close at hand, or hunted.
We ate their venison in hunting season.
Guns were far from my mind when I decided to come
    back,
pregnant with you, after years living on either coast.
People would say Texas? Doesn't everybody have a
    gun?
No, I laughed. Not everybody.

What I thought about when I thought about home
    was wildflowers
rampaging across the land in spring; about fishing in
    shallow bays.
I thought Uvalde would be a name you knew from
    stories I told
of the girl with the snakeskin briefcase.
Or maybe you would know it from driving country
    roads, stopping for tacos.
I hoped you would watch the sky, the hills, as I had,
    and contemplate the possibilities.
Instead, Uvalde will mean something else to you.
It won't feel like a creek-polished stone when you say it.
Uvalde—once a place, now an everlasting trigger. Like
    the others.
We'll drive west in a week's time, as we do when
    summer starts,
across the coastal plains, climbing gradually into the
    hills.
We'll watch the clouds, darting, shape-shifting, like
    children playing tag,
their shadows mingling on the ground below.

馬爾法的頭一個早晨
First Morning in West Texas

LAO YANG

雞叫三遍之後
汽車和火車都醒了

人還睡著

After three crows of the rooster
Cars wake up and the train as well

People still sleep

April Snow

MATTHEW ZAPRUDER

Today in El Paso all the planes are asleep on the
    runway. The world
is in a delay. All the political consultants drinking
    whiskey keep
their heads down, lifting them only to look at the
    beautiful scarred
waitress who wears typewriter keys as a necklace. They
    jingle
when she brings them drinks. Outside the giant plate
    glass windows
the planes are completely covered in snow, it piles up
    on the wings.
I feel like a mountain of cell phone chargers. Each of
    the various
faiths of our various fathers keeps us only partly
    protected. I don't
want to talk on the phone to an angel. At night before
    I go to sleep
I am already dreaming. Of coffee, of ancient generals,
    of the faces
of statues each of which has the eternal expression of
    one of my feelings.

I examine my feelings without feeling anything. I ride
   my blue bike
on the edge of the desert. I am president of this glass
   of water.

Jenny Browne is a professor of English and creative writing at Trinity University. Her most recent poetry collection is *Fellow Travelers: New and Selected Poems*. A former James Michener fellow at the University of Texas, she has received the Cecil Hemley Memorial Award from the Poetry Society of America, a National Endowment for the Arts poetry fellowship, and two literature fellowships from the Texas Writers League. Her poems and essays have appeared most recently in the *American Poetry Review*, the *Oxford American*, *Poetry Magazine*, the *Nation*, and the *New York Times*. She served concurrent terms as the 2016–18 poet laureate of San Antonio and the 2017 poet laureate of Texas, and she was the 2019–20 and 2023–24 Distinguished Fulbright Scholar at the Seamus Heaney Centre in Belfast, Northern Ireland. She was inducted into the Texas Institute of Letters in 2023. She lives in San Antonio.